Intellectual Jazz II

Books by Keith N. Ferreira

The Intellectual Rebel
Aphorisms
Speculative Aphorisms
Speculative Aphorisms II
Philoscience
Philoscience II
Intellectual Jazz
Intellectual Jazz II

Please visit my website at: Philophysics.com. Thank you!

Intellectual Jazz II

Keith N. Ferreira

iUniverse, Inc.
New York Lincoln Shanghai

Intellectual Jazz II

iUniverse, Inc.

For information address:
iUniverse, Inc.
2021 Pine Lake Road, Suite 100
Lincoln, NE 68512
www.iuniverse.com

ISBN: 0-595-28158-3

Printed in the United States of America

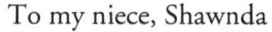

To my niece, Shawnda

Contents

Part One

Philosophy

Philosophy is the former name of philoscience.

Science

Science is a form of intellectual activity that investigates nature.

Nature

There are no problems that nature cannot and has not solved, because nature has zero entropy.

Evolution and Progress

Evolution and progress are moving the universe towards zero entropy, despite what scientists state to the contrary.

Not Sacrosanct

I believe that nobody's ideas are sacrosanct, nor should they be believed to be sacrosanct.

Some Ideas

Some ideas develop such momentum, because of their influence, that they remain influential long after they have outlasted their usefulness.

Different and Separate

IQ, academic proficiency, creativity, and talent are four different and separate things, and besides that, there are many different and separate kinds of creativity and talent. So that one can have one kind of creativity or talent, and not others. Also, one can have a high IQ and be academically nonproficient as I am.

A Broad Spectrum

The fate of a country should not be in the hands of one or a few individuals, but it should be in the hands of a broad spectrum of individuals and institutions.

Neanderthals and Chimps

The leaders of Third World countries are mostly Neanderthals, and their followers and supporters are mostly chimps, because they are politically and intellectually bankrupt.

Productivity and Creativity

An important future development in employment is that employees will be paid based on their productivity and creativity, and not on their ranks within the organizations that they work for.

An Idea

There is nothing that crystallizes an idea in the mind better than finding the right words to express the idea.

Being Profound

When most intellectuals and academics are being profound, they are usually parroting the ideas, if not the words of some living or dead original thinker.

Highly Intelligent People

Highly intelligent people are seldom intellectually creative. There ought to be a word that mean intellectually creative to distinguish it from the word intelligent. I suggest the word "intellecative" should be used to mean intellectually creative.

Creative Thought

Philoscience requires a great deal of creative thought, and that is why philoscience will require great thinkers. One should not confuse intellectual creativity with intelligence, because intelligence is academic competence, and academic competence does not require intellectual creativity.

Experts

Experts still believe in in-groups and out-groups, and they also still believe in the exclusivity of in-groups. This just goes to show how far behind the times they are.

Information

With the explosion in the volume of information in recent times, the aphorism will become the ideal means of communication, because it is concise and to the point.

A Unified Field Theory

A unified field theory only makes sense if all the fields of force of nature are unified into one field of force and that unified field of force is the gravitational field of force. That is exactly what the theory of fundamentons does.

Theory of Fundamentons

The theory of fundamentons is the unified field theory that physicists are seeking, although my theory of fundamentons is not what physicists were expecting. Physicists were expecting that the different fields of force would coexist in the unified field particles, but that is not how my theory has turned out.

The Ancient Greeks

If Americans would like to be like the ancient Greeks, then Americans must use grease (Greece), because Greek is up the ass.

Scientists and Philosophers

Most scientists and philosophers are so arrogant and bigoted that they believe that a scientific or philosophical outsider cannot make an important contribution to science or philosophy.

History

History is the chronicling of the follies and foibles of human beings.

Philoscientists

I would advise all philoscientists to adopt the aphorism as their mode of communication, because if one cannot express an idea in the form of an aphorism, then one has not fully understood the idea one wishes to express.

Study Neoliberal Arts

If one wants to be a philoscientist, then one should study neoliberal arts, because philoscience is what liberal arts should have been all along. Philoscience is neoliberal arts.

The Interpretation

Philoscience is what liberal arts should have been all along, namely the interpretation and critique of all intellectual activity.

To Religious People

To religious people who ascribe the evils of the modern age to its irreligiosity, I reply to them: how is a religious age any different from an irreligious age? To my mind, there is no difference between a religious age and an irreligious age.

A Religious Age

Why should human beings go back to a religious age? Is a religious age any better than an irreligious age?

Intellectual Chimps

Most blacks are intellectual chimps, because they seldom engage in intellectual pursuits.

One Can Circumvent

If one has money to publish one's own ideas, then one can circumvent the experts, because the experts always have been and always will be obstacles to progress.

To Discover

To discover a new intellectual or academic discipline is to be like an explorer who has discovered a new continent, because everywhere the discoverer looks, there is something new to be discovered.

Not Sciences

Philoscience and its subdisciplines are not sciences, but they are the embodiment of neoliberal arts. In other words, philoscience is neoliberal arts.

To Seek Knowledge

When I was a child, I wanted to go to school to seek knowledge, but I was sadly disappointed when I started to go to school, because schools are not organized to impart knowledge. Instead, schools are organized for students who wish to compete against each other for good grades and academic credentials.

The Only Way

The only way to seek knowledge is to educate oneself, because academia is not organized to impart knowledge, but instead, academia is organized to make students compete against each other for good grades and academic credentials.

Biositology

Biositology is the study of the parasitic nature of life. All living organisms are biosites. A biositologist is anyone who studies the parasitic nature of life.

All Human Activity

All human activity is biositic, because human beings are biosites like all other living organisms.

Psychositology

Psychositology is the study of the parasitic nature of the mind, and a psychosite is a conscious mind. Psychositology is a fact that cannot be denied.

Physicositology

Physicositology is the study of the parasitic nature of nonliving matter and energy, and a physicosite is a nonliving entity. Physicositology is a fact of nature that cannot be denied.

Archaeologists

Archaeologists should be careful when they unearth the remains of ancient civilizations, because they could unearth some monster idea that could have destroyed the ancient culture and could destroy modern civilization, too.

Theositology

Theositology is the study of the parasitic nature of God, and a theosite is a god. Theositology is a fact that cannot be denied.

A Major Branch

Economics is one of the major branches of biositology. Biositology is a fact of nature that cannot be denied.

The Nature of Slavery

Biositology explains the nature of slavery and all forms of human exploitation.

Genius

Genius is like unshaped blocks of mental marble, because one has to chisel away intellectually at the mental marble in order to release the genius forms that lie hidden within the mental marble.

Black Holes and White Holes

Scientists are hotly debating about whether or not there are black holes and white holes in the universe, but I know for a fact that there are black holes and white holes in the universe, because black women have black holes, and white women have white holes.

Not Intelligent

I do not consider myself to be intelligent, but I do consider myself to be intellectually creative or intellecative.

Creativity vs. Intelligence

It is better to be creative than to be intelligent, because intelligence produces nothing new, while creativity produces new stuff. However, most academics prefer intelligence to creativity in their students.

Organized Structurally

The way an organization is organized structurally determines the kind of communication structure it will have. That is to say that how an organization is organized structurally will determine whether it will communicate internally along nonneural logic circuitry lines or along neural network logic circuitry lines.

Usually Due

Organizational failures and breakdowns of organizations are usually due to the adoption of nonneural logic circuitry organizational structures and internal communication by organizations.

The Prefix Philo-

When the prefix philo- is affixed to any intellectual discipline or activity, it comes under the domain of philoscience.

From Time to Time

From time to time, I indulge in philopolitics, philoeconomics, philosociology, and other philos, but my main love is philophysics and philophilosophy.

Academics and Intellectuals

Most academics and intellectuals are intelligent, but are not intellecative, while most geniuses are intellecative, but not intelligent.

Intellecative

It is better to be intellecative than to be intelligent, but most academics seem to disagree with me, because they do not appreciate intellecative students who are not intelligent.

To Build Anything

To build anything, one has to destroy something else, because that is the nature of existence.

Theory and Practice

Politically, economically, culturally, and sociologically speaking, the further apart theory and practice are, the more backward and corrupt the society.

Human Beings

Human beings do not need to worship or pray to God, because God never said he needed us to worship or pray to him. In fact, God never spoke a word to human beings.

Genius

Genius is not high intelligence. Instead, genius is high intellecativity, which means high intellectual creativity.

Theoretical Physicists

Theoretical physicists are equation manipulators and poor thinkers. Experimental physicists are better thinkers than theoretical physicists, because experimental physics requires a great deal of thought, while theoretical physics requires the manipulation of mathematical symbols according to logical rules.

Mathematicians and Logicians

I do not consider most mathematicians and logicians to be great thinkers, because most mathematicians and logicians are human computers, and computers are as dumb as an ox.

The Strange Beliefs

The strange beliefs of cultures all around the world should not surprise anyone, because all human beings are groping in the intellectual dark for the meaning of life and one's reason for being.

Existence

Existence must have a purpose, because zero has zero entropy, which means that zero is all wise.

Macroeconomics

A nation's economy is no longer macroeconomics, because the world's economy is now macroeconomics. A nation's economy is now mesoeconomics.

Microeconomics

The economics of large corporations and all smaller entities should be called microeconomics.

All Leaders

All leaders are con-artists, and that is why they must be controlled, because leadership is a necessary con-game.

Neoliberal Arts

Neoliberal arts will be a great intellectual and academic discipline, if neoliberal arts is not taught as gospel, but is allowed to be questioned and made contributions to.

Professionals

Professionals who ignore my books do so at their own and their country's peril.

Lack Substantive Content

Most well written books lack substantive content. In fact, most books lack substantive content.

Physical Phenomena

One does not understand physical phenomena until one can visualize physical phenomena, despite what physicists state to the contrary.

Will Be Discovered

Someday, equations describing the behavior of micropolitics, mesopolitics, and macropolitics will be discovered. Micropolitics is state and local politics, mesopolitics is national politics, and macropolitics is world politics.

The Physical Universe

The physical universe is a form of virtual reality that is validated by the mind. In fact, the physical universe is empty, except for conscious minds. However, the physical universe is the rationale for all conscious minds in our universe.

Virtual Reality

Because zero has zero entropy, it means that zero is the realm of perfect, ultimate, and absolute science, intrinsically. And that is why the physical universe can be virtual reality and still be the rationale behind the conscious mind.

Equations

Someday, there will be equations that describe the behavior of human cultures. In fact, someday, there will be equations for everything in nature, including history.

Written Words

The beauty of written words is in their meanings and not in any poetic effects that they might be put to. Poets do not seem to understand this.

Quantifiable Knowledge

Quantifiable knowledge is the most useful kind of knowledge, but it isn't the most profound kind of knowledge. Philoscientific knowledge is the most profound kind of knowledge possible.

Most Poets

Most poets are intellectual chimps, because their poetry lacks substantive content. Most poetry reminds me of elaborately decorated useless devices.

A Misconception

It is a misconception that liberal arts students cannot make important contributions to knowledge, because philoscience, which is the new name for liberal arts, can and is making important contributions to the advancement of knowledge.

Talented Philoscientists

Talented philoscientists of the future will be on the cutting edge of knowledge, although they will be generalists and not specialists.

Virtual Reality

Virtual reality means to appear to be real from the perspective of the mind, but to be, in fact, nonexistent or unreal.

The Mind

The mind is real, but the meaning of its contents might or might not be true. The mind is the only yardstick with which to judge reality.

One of the Greatest

One of the greatest contributions to culture is the demystification of all religions, because all religions are curses upon the earth.

The Advancement of Knowledge

One of my greatest contributions to the advancement of knowledge is my effort to demystify God and Christ.

Black Parents

Black parents are partly responsible for the paucity of black students that major in math and science, because they do not encourage their children to study math and science.

Another Reason

Another reason for the paucity of black students that major in math and science is black peer group pressure against studying math and science.

The Expression

The expression "Holy shit!" started when Christ went into the bushes to take a shit. After Christ left the bushes, his disciples went into the bushes, and when they saw Christ's shit, they each took a piece, and they rubbed it in their faces, and then they uttered that famous expression "Holy shit!"

Talking Shit

When I talk shit, I really talk about shit.

Teaching Liberal Arts

The old way of teaching liberal arts will not do for the new discipline of philoscience, because with philoscience, the main emphasis should be placed on intellectual creativity or intellecativity.

High Intellecativity

To be a talented philoscientist, one does not need high intelligence, but one needs high intellecativity.

Has Always Been

The number one problem in the world has always been politics and always will be politics, because human beings are imperfect.

A Solution

If a solution is found to politics, then most other problems will become manageable, but a solution to politics is unlikely.

Informal Groups

Informal groups usually communicate among themselves along neural network logic circuitry lines. Formal groups should communicate internally along similar lines, because nonneural logic circuitry communication is defective.

Corrupt Organizations

Corrupt organizations always adopt nonneural logic circuitry communication, because it is undemocratic and very easy to manipulate for corrupt purposes.

Positions of Authority

Everyone in positions of authority is a con-artist to some degree, because to rise to positions of authority, people have to be con-artists to some degree.

Consummate Con-Artists

Preachers, poets, and politicians are the consummate con-artists, because their con-artistry is overjoyously appreciated by their audiences.

The True Miracle

The true miracle of Christianity is that it has lasted as long as it has, because it is an absurd and ridiculous religion. In fact, all religions are absurd and ridiculous.

I Refuse

I refuse to worship anyone who shit on the earth or shit in the universe.

Most Ph.D.'s

Most Ph.D.'s are highly intelligent, but few Ph.D.'s are highly intellecative. The word intellecative means intellectually creative.

Worth

One highly intellecative person is worth ten thousand Ph.D.'s.

Sociologically Speaking

Sociologically speaking, organizations of all kinds should be organized like simple neural network logic circuitry, and not like nonneural logic circuits, because neural network logic circuitry is more like how human beings think than nonneural logic circuits.

Most Organizations

Most organizations today are organized along nonneural logic circuitry lines, but that is not the best way to organize the structure of organizations. The best way to organize the structure of organizations is along neural network logic circuitry lines.

Philopoetry and Philoreligion

Philopoetry is the interpretation and critique of poetry, while philoreligion is the interpretation and critique of religion. All philos are interpretations and critiques of the subjects they belong to.

I Have to Admit

I have to admit that I indulge a lot in philopoetry and philoreligion, because there is so much I dislike about poetry and religion.

My Philoscientific Thinking

I do most of my philoscientific thinking while listening to music on the radio and reading poetry all at the same time. I hate poetry, but it helps me to think. Most poetry is so anti-intellectual, anti-science, and anti-technology, that I think that poets are intellectual chimps.

Hallucinating

People who find profound meanings in poetry are hallucinating, because most poetry is moronic.

It is Much Better

It is much better to be creative than to be intelligent, but academics emphasize intelligence and ignore creativity. Intelligence and creativity are two distinct faculties of the human mind. When will academics understand this?

Talented People

There are many talented people who are not intelligent that are being ignored around the world. My purpose in life is to help these people to become recognized.

Artisticativity

Artisticativity means artistic creativity. Many people are artisticative, but are not intelligent. Artisticative people who are not intelligent are another group of people who are ignored around the world.

The Reason Why

The reason why I know that intelligence and creativity are two different things is because I have studied myself over the past fifty-one years, and I have come to the conclusion that I am intellecative, but not intelligent.

Intellecative Students

Academics love intelligent students and despise intellecative students. I would rather be intellecative than intelligent any day.

My Purpose in Life

My purpose in life is to promote and popularize the plight of intellecative persons all around the world. Intellecative people are being ignored all around the world.

Hegel

If one does not philosophize in the manner of Hegel, then one is a philosophical and intellectual minnow.

Like Hegel

To philosophize like Hegel does not mean to adopt his writing or expositional style, but it means to be comprehensive and have philosophical depth.

Mental Perceptions

Mental perceptions occur exactly where they are perceived in the mind, and they do not occur in some physical brain, which is part of virtual reality. However, mental perceptions do have physical effects in the virtual brain.

All Mental Phenomena

All mental phenomena are associated with some kind of physical phenomena, no matter how subtle the mental phenomena, but that does not mean that physical reality is not virtual reality. In fact, physical reality is virtual reality. On the other hand, mental reality is as real as reality can ever be.

Nature

Nature is literally nothing without consciousness.

Only Conscious Minds

Only conscious minds can deny the existence of the conscious mind and be conscious of doing so.

It is Possible

It is possible to explain nature using metaphors of ordinary experience, and that is why nature is an open-book test and not a closed-book test, because anyone can read the book of nature by creating metaphors that shed light on the nature of reality.

Ordinary Metaphors

Because anyone can create ordinary metaphors that shed light on the nature of reality, it means that science will never be beyond the understanding of the average person, despite what most scientists believe.

Most Scientists

Most scientists are intellectual bovines, because they have herdlike mentalities.

Intellectual Bovines

People should have fun lassoing scientists, because most scientists are intellectual bovines.

Feelings and Impressions

Before ideas are articulated and expressed by an individual, they are vague feelings and impressions in the individual's mind.

Intellectual Outsiders

Intellectual outsiders have always, and will always, make important contributions to the advancement of knowledge, despite their outsider status. Intellectual insiders will never learn this truth.

Should Try to Make

Philoscientists can and should try to make contributions to all branches of theoretical knowledge, because that is what intellectual generality is all about.

Is Not Science

Philoscience is not science nor is it a science. Instead, philoscience is neoliberal arts.

The Laws of Nature

Even the laws of nature are exploitative and parasitic. This just goes to underscore the fact that all aspects of nature are exploitative and parasitic.

Sitology

Sitology is the study of the exploitative and parasitic nature of all aspects of nature, including God.

The Goal

The goal of every creative intellectual is to intellectually culture or cultivate colonies or groups of followers that will perpetuate and propagate his or her theories and ideas.

Human Beings

Human beings are culturephiles, because they love to belong to or form different kinds of cultures. For instance, human beings love to belong to racial, ethnic, religious, political, social, and many other kinds of cultures.

Money

Money is the blood of society, and everyone in society engages in monetary or blood transactions.

Exploit and Feed

Economics is the study of how people exploit and feed off each other.

The Myth

The myth of the human being is one of the most successful myths in all of history.

Are Subhuman

All human beings are subhuman, because human beings are religiously inspired myths.

I Do Not Believe

I do not believe that anyone is intellectually special, because I believe that anyone can make important contributions to the advancement of knowledge.

Most Professionals

Most professionals are intellectual bigots, because they believe that advanced academic degrees make them intellectually special.

My Main Message

My main message to the world is that one can make important contributions to the advancement of knowledge without advanced academic degrees. This has always been true, and will always be true, despite what academics state to the contrary.

Religion

Religion is such an effective means of brainwashing that it can take some people their whole lives to free themselves from under its spell. Most people never get freed from under its spell.

High Scores

High scores on standardized academic tests do not mean a damn thing, except to academics, because the world of academia is a world of fantasy.

I Am Opposed

I am opposed to standardized academic tests, because academic errors and falsehoods become standardized and because standardization of academic tests stifles creativity and originality.

Standardized Tests

Standardized tests are a tool of exploitation by those in power who wish to accomplish their narrow agendas.

The Main Problem

The main problem with the standardization of anything to do with knowledge is that it standardizes errors or falsehoods along with the truth.

Blacks

I do not expect blacks to embrace my ideas, because they do not know how to recognize intellectual talent. If blacks knew how to recognize intellectual talent, then Africa would not be so backward.

My Hope

My hope in writing my books is that I hope that I will inspire other talented people to persevere, although they might not be intelligent, because intelligence is highly overrated.

The U.S. Government

The U.S. government knows that I am a genius, because they told me so and because I helped them during the Vietnam, Watergate, and Cold War crises. My experiment over the past thirty years was a resounding success, because no one embraced me or my ideas.

The U.S. Congress

The U.S. Congress has my Ph.D. that I got in 1972. I told the Congress to keep my Ph.D. for me so that I can carry out an experiment. My experiment was to discover what happens to most geniuses in society.

In 1975

In 1975, a professor at City College asked me if I wanted all the Nobel Prizes for 1975, and I told him no, because I said that I am getting a lot of ideas while at the bottom, so why should I move to the top.

In 1980

In 1980, a VA staff member told me that I have about twelve Ph.D.'s.

Part Two

In No Way Unusual

Bose-Einstein condensates (BEC) are caused by special suspension forces and are in no way unusual.

Cooper Pairs

The idea of "Cooper pairs" of electrons in superconductor physics is absolute nonsense, because "Cooper pairs" are figments of the imaginations of physicists.

The Maximum Acceleration

$a_{max} < (c/s)$, where a_{max} equals the maximum acceleration possible in the universe, c equals the velocity of light in a vacuum, and s equals one second.

The Acceleration Factor

$\sqrt{1-a^2/(c/s)^2}$, is the acceleration factor, where a equals the acceleration of an object, c equals the velocity of light in a vacuum, and s equals one second.

Do Not Collapse

Probability waves do not collapse just because quantum particles have definite locations, because quantum particles always have definite locations, although they teleport from point to point within their probability waves.

Can and Do

Probability waves can and do influence each other instantaneously over any physical distance.

Synergics

The country that develops the science of synergics first will control the world. Synergics is the science that combines quantum randomness and electronic logic circuitry to form synergic technology.

Theoretical Science

There are basically two kinds of theoretical science: metaphorical theoretical science and realistic theoretical science. Both are useful, but only realistic theoretical science is true.

Realistic Physics Theory

Realistic physics theory is being transformed more and more into metaphorical physics theory. In other worlds, physics is sliding down a slippery slope into scientific oblivion.

Physicists

Physicists should spend their time making metaphorical physics theory into more realistic physics theory.

Physics Theory

Any physics theory that is more fundamental than quark theory is likely to be metaphorical and not realistic, because quarks are probably realistically fundamental, and any theory more fundamental is likely to be metaphorically fundamental and not realistically fundamental.

The Theory of Quarks

The theory of quarks is half metaphorical and half realistic, because quarks probably exist, but gluons are unlikely to exist.

The Quantum Level

On the quantum level, certain portions of probability waves atrophy and die long before their probability waves collapse completely.

The More Massive

The more massive an object is, the shorter the time interval before its probability wave collapses naturally.

Suspension Forces

Physicists do not believe in suspension forces as yet, but someday soon they will believe in suspension forces, because suspension forces are real forces.

In Atoms

In atoms, electrons, protons, and neutrons are governed by standing probability waves, such that their cores teleport from point to point within the atoms, although their electric charges, in the case of electrons and protons, are held stationary by suspension forces in the atoms.

A Simple Equation

A simple equation that describes the nature of fundamental particles in general is waiting to be discovered.

To Be Discovered

A simple equation that describes the nature of chemicals in general is waiting to be discovered.

Three Kinds

There are basically three kinds of mass/energy in physics: kinetic mass/energy, rest mass/energy, and potential mass/energy. Rest and kinetic mass/energy are self-explanatory, but potential mass/energy is mass/energy that has the potential to exist, but does not exist as yet.

Permanent Magnetism

Permanent magnetism is not due to charges in motion, but is due to the physical structure and nature of the interior of certain kinds of atoms.

Not Completely Valid

It is probably valid to state that no conservation law of nature is completely valid.

Sheds Light

The simple equation waiting to be discovered that sheds light on the nature of chemicals in general will also shed light on the simple equation waiting to be discovered that sheds light on the nature of fundamental particles, in general. Whichever is discovered first will shed light on the other.

Under Certain Conditions

Under certain conditions, like in Bose-Einstein condensates, for instance, probability waves can behave coherently. Another example is the probability waves of laser light.

When Colonies

When colonies of probability waves are behaving coherently, it means that the quantum spins associated with the quantum particles whose probability waves are behaving coherently are also behaving coherently.

Time

Time might not be quantized after all, because there are no good reasons why it should be quantized.

Behave Coherently

The electrons that comprise the electric currents in superconductors behave coherently when the superconductors are superconducting.

Quantum Mechanics

Quantum mechanics with the correct modifications can endure for a very long time, indeed.

To Influence

To influence quantum particles is to influence the probabilities of the probability waves of quantum particles.

Quantum Particle Tunneling

Quantum particle tunneling is actually a result of the teleportism of quantum particles within their probability waves.

Behave as Though

Probability waves behave as though their quantum particles are everywhere within their probability waves, but in fact, that is not the case.

Space and Time

People who believe that space and time are quantized do so because they lack imagination.

I Once Believed

I once believed that time is quantized, because I lacked the conviction of my imagination.

Fields of Force

Fields of force are one of the ways by which one can influence the probabilities of probability waves of quantum particles. Another way is by contact forces, a third way is by special environmental factors, and a fourth way is by synergic effects.

Will Be Disproven

Virtual and exchange particles are ideas that will be disproven some time in this century.

I Am Certain

I am certain that the acceleration factor, $\sqrt{1 - a^2/(c/s)^2}$, plays a part in determining the effects of the uncertainty principle of quantum mechanics.

The Teleportistic Interpretation

The teleportistic interpretation of quantum mechanics is much simpler and much more believable than the Copenhagen interpretation of quantum mechanics.

Has Reached a Point

Fundamental particle physics has reached a point where it is producing diminishing returns. Condense matter physics is probably the new frontier of physics.

A Scientific Wasteland

The general theory of relativity has led physics into a scientific wasteland from which it will have to retreat if physics is to survive.

The Fundamenton

I call the most fundamental particle the fundamenton, and it is theoretically possible that it is real, but it probably never existed in the universe, and probably never will exist in the universe, because the energy needed to create it probably cannot be concentrated in particle collisions.

Massive Stellar Objects

If fundamentons exist, they will be concentrated in extremely massive stellar objects.

Photons

Photons are particles that behave like waves, because they oscillate back and forth perpendicular to the direction of motion as they travel at the velocity of light.

Rest Mass

Rest mass consists of a kind of photonlike particles that oscillate back and forth inside the cores of fundamental particles.

A Teleforce

A teleforce is a force that acts at a distance. Gravity, suspension forces, and synergic forces are all teleforces, because they act at a distance, and they are all instantaneous forces.

Telephenomena

Telephenomena are phenomena that are mediated by teleforces. Probability waves are mediated, coordinated, and collapsed by teleforces.

Physically Speaking

Physically speaking, it is impossible to push the idea of consciousness beyond the statement that consciousness is a special kind of agglomeration of nonclassical probability waves.

At Best

At best, a special kind of agglomeration of probability waves represents virtual consciousness, because the conscious mind is not a special kind of physical reality, but is a special kind of nonphysical reality, although the conscious mind does occupy space and time.

Are Not Relative

The frequencies of free energy waves are not relative, but they are intrinsic. However, the interaction frequencies of free energy waves are relative to the velocities of their interaction partners.

Free Energy Waves

Free energy waves interact with each other relative to their intrinsic frequencies.

Massive Starlike Objects

Fundamenton stars are massive starlike objects that consist of fundamentons. The temperature of most fundamenton stars are probably close to absolute zero, because the only motion inside these stars is due to the quantum agitation produced by standing probability waves of the fundamentons in the stars.

Fundamentons Consist

Fundamentons consist of dimensionless particles that oscillate back and forth, such that they give rise to rest mass. Fundamentons decay into less fundamental particles when they are free. Fundamentons are so simple that they have no quantum numbers.

Not Possible in Nature

Fundamenton stars are not black holes, because black holes are not possible in nature.

Probably Concentrated

All the matter in fundamenton stars are probably concentrated in a volume smaller than that of a neutron, because all fundamentons in fundamenton stars are superimposed on each other.

Physical Concepts

Physicists need to constantly update their physical concepts, because most physical concepts more than ten years old are likely to be outdated.

Gravitational Singularities

Gravitational singularities are impossible, because rest mass consists of the back and forth oscillation of photonlike particles in the cores of fundamental particles. A gravitational singularity would have zero mass, because there would be no room for the photonlike cores of particles to oscillate.

The End

The end of fundamental particle physics is in sight, because fundamentons are the end of the road for fundamental particle physics.

Photons Lose Energy

Photons lose energy so gradually as they age that their loss of energy is imperceptible in a person's lifetime.

The Early Universe

The early universe did not contain fundamentons. Instead, the early universe contained neutrons and photons dispersed throughout the universe.

Their Own Antiparticles

Fundamentons are their own antiparticles, just like photons are their own anti-particles.

Combined

In the early universe, some protons which formed from the decay of some neutrons combined with some neutrons that did not decay to form the nuclei of deuterium, tritium, helium, and even lithium.

Decay Into Quarks

Fundamentons decay into quarks, because fundamentons are more fundamental than quarks. It might be possible to create fundamentons in particle accelerators.

Do Not Exist

Virtual and exchange particles do not exist, despite what physicists state to the contrary.

Is Not Expanding

The universe is not expanding, despite what physicists state to the contrary.

Started Out

The universe started out with maximum entropy, despite what physicists state to the contrary.

Gradually Approaching

The universe is gradually approaching zero entropy, despite what physicists state to the contrary.

Atmospheric Mesons

Atmospheric mesons live longer than laboratory mesons, because atmospheric mesons experience the density effect to a greater extent, because of their high velocity, and they also experience deceleration. Both of these phenomena slow the flow of time.

It Might Be Possible

It might be possible to make semiconductor diodes behave as heat-to-electricity converters by heating the diodes, while electric or magnetic fields are applied across the pn junctions of the diodes.

Denser Than

I call stars denser than quark stars fundamenton stars. Fundamenton stars are the densest stars possible, because any star denser than a quark star is a fundamenton star.

In One Star

If all the matter in the universe were concentrated in one star, it still would not form a black hole, but it will form a fundamenton star, because it requires an infinite amount of mass/energy to form a black hole.

Quarks and Antiquarks

Fundamentons decay into quarks and antiquarks, because fundamentons are their own antiparticles.

Are Distinctly Different

Standing probability waves are distinctly different from kinetic probability waves.

Time Flow

Time flow is relative to acceleration and gravity, but is not relative to velocity as the theory of relativity states.

Distance or Length

Distance or length is a vector quantity that is dependent on the light vector and the velocity of the object whose distance or length is to be measured.

The Intrinsic Frequency

The intrinsic frequency of the probability standing wave of a quantum object is given by the equation: f=E/h, where f is the intrinsic frequency of the probability standing wave of a quantum object, E equals the rest energy of the quantum object, and h equals Planck's constant.

Semi-Independent

The cores of fundamental particles are semi-independent of their electric and magnetic fields, because the cores of fundamental particles teleport from point to point within their probability waves without affecting the locations or behavior of their electric or magnetic fields.

Theoretical Physics

Theoretical physics started to go awry when James Clerk Maxwell developed his electromagnetic theory of light, and it has continued to go awry ever since.

Nonnaive Common Sense

Theoretical physics began to go awry as soon as it abandoned using nonnaive common sense and started relying on the manipulation of mathematical symbols.

The Greatest Flaw

The greatest flaw of nature is that in order to create anything, one has to destroy something else.

The Results

The results of the experimental sciences are subtle enough that they are fueling the erroneous imaginations of scientists of all kinds. Only philoscience can keep the erroneous imaginations of scientists in check.

Reasoning Correctly

Philophysics can assist physics in reasoning correctly about physics, because philophysics provides a critique of physics that physics needs badly.

Chemists

Chemists will not obtain an adequate equation for molecules and materials, in general, until they include suspension forces in their equations, because suspension forces play a part in all of chemistry.

Synergic Metamorphosis

Synergic manufacturing is a form of manufacturing whereby one puts useless material into a synergic manufacturing device and out comes a finished and new consumer product by means of synergic metamorphosis.

Trial and Error

Synergic technology is a trial and error type of technology, because one cannot get far with synergic theory alone.

Indefinitely

With synergic technology, people will be able to live youthful and healthy lives indefinitely.

Synergic Manufacturing

Synergic manufacturing is possible with synergic technology. Synergic manufacturing will be possible in the next hundred years or so.

Synergic Technology

Synergic technology is the most advanced technology possible.

The Cosmosphere

The cosmosphere is an impenetrable barrier that surrounds the universe.

Virtual Bodies

People are not their physical bodies, but they are their minds. Anyway, physical bodies are virtual bodies and not real bodies, because the physical universe is virtual reality.

Reality

The conscious mind is reality, and it is the only reality human beings will ever experience on this side of death.

Space and Time

Space and time are not quantized, despite what physicists state to the contrary.

Permanent Magnetism

Even to this day, permanent magnetism is little understood, because permanent magnetism is not due to electric charges in motion, but is due to the intrinsic structure of certain atoms.

The Nuclei

Perhaps the nuclei of certain atoms do not spin when they absorb photons.

All Quantum Particles

All quantum particles with rest mass possess standing probability waves.

Special Influence

Matter, energy, fields of force, and probability waves consist of areas of special influence that influence other areas of special influence.

Areas of

Areas of special influence consist of matter, energy, fields of force, and probability waves.

The Most Massive

Fundamentons are the most massive fundamental particles in the universe.

Dimensionless Particle

Fundamentons are dimensionless particles that oscillate back and forth, such that their oscillations give rise to their rest mass.

Simplest Particle Possible

The fundamenton is the simplest particle possible, because it has no quantum numbers, is a neutral particle, and it decays into quarks.

Created in Stars

Fundamentons are created in stars more massive than quark stars. Fundamenton stars are the end of the line for stars, because there are no black holes, despite what physicists state to the contrary.

Antientropism

Antientropism is the principle that states that the universe is decreasing in entropy, instead of increasing in entropy, despite what physicists state to the contrary.

The Anthropic Principle

The anthrophic principle makes sense, because nature is deterministic, and the universe is antientropistic, which means that the universe is decreasing in entropy.

The Principle of Teleportism

Because of the principle of teleportism, to be at rest relative to a kinetic probability wave is not to be at rest relative to its quantum particle, since the quantum particle can still teleport from point to point within its standing and kinetic probability waves.

Quantum Objects

Quantum objects are never at rest, because of their standing probability waves.

A Truly Fundamental Particle

f=E/hA, where f equals the frequency of the core of a truly fundamental particle, E equals the rest energy of a truly fundamental particle, h equals Planck's constant, and A equals the amplitude factor of the oscillations at the core of the truly fundamental particle.

Smallest and Most Massive

Fundamenton stars are the smallest and the most massive stars in the universe, because the size of a fundamenton star is smaller than the size of a neutron and is more massive than a quark star.

Zero and Infinity

Zero and infinity are divine numbers or beings, because they have zero entropy.

The Jazzon

Another name for the fundamenton is the jazzon. It is befitting that jazz has put the capstone on fundamental particle physics.

Fields of Influence

Fields of force are nothing more nor less than fields of influence, because fields of force are fields of influence. In other words, matter and energy are nothing more nor less than fields of influence.

Dynamic or Static

Fields of influence are either dynamic or static and instantaneous or noninstantaneous.

A New Theory

A new theory of entropy needs to be developed, because the old theory of entropy is wrong or is misapplied.

The Classical Theory

The classical theory of entropy when it is applied to cosmology is dead, because it is wrong, since entropy is not increasing in the universe as a whole, but is decreasing.

Chance

The universe did not have to rely on chance to get it going, despite what cosmologists state to the contrary, because zero has zero entropy, or perfect order, will, and knowledge.

The Purpose of

The purpose of the universe is to go from maximum entropy to minimum entropy. In other words, the purpose of the universe is to express evolution.

Fundamental Asymmetry

There is a fundamental asymmetry on the most fundamental level of nature, because jazzons decay into much more matter than antimatter.

Could Have Existed

Jazzons could have existed at the origin of the universe after all, because jazzons decay into much more matter than antimatter, which is consistent with the preponderance of matter over antimatter in the universe.

Under Certain Conditions

Under certain conditions, like in quantum superposition states, for instance, standing probability waves can become distorted, and the quantum particle associated with this probability wave distortion seems to be in more than one place at once, but this is merely an illusion caused by teleportism.

Standing Probability Waves

Protons, neutrons, and electrons in atoms do not have kinetic probability waves, but they do have standing probability waves.

In Physics

In physics, mathematical brilliance is a sideshow, because it tends to be Ptolemaic. Physicists should remember that nature is simple but profound and not complicated and pointless.

Too Complicated

Quantum mechanics, the general theory of relativity, and superstring theory are too complicated to be true. Therefore, they are Ptolemaic. Theoretical physics is being fooled by its mathematical brilliance, but that is what Ptolemaicism is all about.

Photons

Photons do not have standing probability waves, but they do have kinetic probability waves.

Teleforces

Teleforces are instantaneous forces, and there are many different kinds of teleforces in nature.

So Blinded

Physicists are so blinded by the brilliance of their mathematics that they cannot see that entropy is decreasing in the universe.

The Omniscience

The omniscience of the universe does not reside in matter and energy, but it resides in zero, because zero has zero entropy.

Under Certain Conditions

Under certain conditions, like in laser light or in Bose-Einstein condensates, probability waves can behave coherently.

Behave Coherently

When probability waves behave coherently, their quantum particles behave coherently also.

Chance and Randomness

Chance and randomness are impossible, despite what physicists state to the contrary.

Time and Motion

Time and motion are not relative, despite what physicists state to the contrary.

The Frontiers of Knowledge

The frontiers of knowledge are like unexplored jungles, because there are all kinds of monster ideas on the frontiers of knowledge.

Religion

Religion is a con-game in which those that are being conned are eager to be conned.

Fall Into the Trap

It is very easy for intellectuals and academics to fall into the trap of believing that they are expressing profound truths when, in fact, they are expressing absolute crap.

Should Adopt

Intellectuals and academics should adopt the philoscientific method of communication, because if one cannot express oneself philoscientifically, then one probably does not understand what one is expressing.

One of the Tasks

One of the tasks of philoscience is to critique all of the sciences, as well as knowledge in general.

Artificial Barriers

Intellectuals and academics are busy erecting artificial barriers to the acquisition of knowledge, while philoscientists are busy knocking down artificial barriers to the acquisition of knowledge.

Linguistics

The study of linguistics can inform one about the proper uses of language, but it cannot inform one about what to think, believe, or create, how to behave, or what is true or false.

At Best

At best, linguistics is a language tool. At worst, it is a form of intellectual nit-picking.

Been Absent From

Nonnaive common sense has been absent from theoretical physics for too long a period now.

Only Philophysics

Only philophysics can prevent theoretical physics from engaging in sheer folly, because experimental physics is so subtle that it fuels the erroneous imaginations of theoretical physicists.

Last Interaction

The nature of and intrinsic frequency of the kinetic probability wave of a quantum object depends on the nature of its last interaction with matter or energy.

The Cores

The cores of truly fundamental particles with rest mass oscillate back and forth, such that they describe sine waves when their oscillations are plotted against time.

The Physical Manifestations

Nonclassical probability waves are the physical manifestations of life and consciousness in the universe.

Pro-Evolutionary Forces

Pro-evolutionary forces are superior to nonevolutionary or anti-evolutionary forces, because entropy is decreasing in the universe, and that is desirable.

Fundamental Nature

Fundamental nature, which is zero, is probability on autopilot, because fundamental nature does not have anything new to learn, since zero knows everything already.

The Basic Characteristics

The basic characteristics of the conscious mind are givens that cannot be analyzed any further.

The American Revolution

The American Revolution will never be completely over as long as there is injustice in the universe.

Space Pirates

Someday, there will be space pirates, because as long as there are geniuses in the universe, there will always be pirates.

Male Sex Hormone

Geniuses have higher levels of male sex hormone in their blood than normal, especially when they are going through a creative period in their lives.

The Mind Reacts

The mind reacts immunologically to ideas in an analogous manner to the immunological responses of white blood cells to foreign substances.

The World

The world is now a biological laboratory for interdisciplinary biologists.

A Worldwide Conspiracy

In the twentieth century, there was a great worldwide conspiracy among academia to destroy the minds of creative people, because students were taught to answer questions automatically without thinking up the answers.

No Respect

Nature has no respect for human beings, because all that nature has respect for are the laws of nature.

Zero and Infinity

Zero and infinity are Divine numbers or entities, because they both have zero entropy.

In Any Rat Race

In any rat race, the rats are bound to win, because rat races are designed for rats.

I Would Give

If I had my way, I would give every newborn baby a Ph.D., because the rat race to get Ph.D.'s is just that: a rat race.

People Might Wonder

People might wonder how an inch can have as many dimensionless points as a mile, and they might also wonder how a second can have as many dimensionless instants as an hour: well, this can be explained by the equation, $0 \times \infty = x$, where x equals anything possible, and 0 equals any dimensionless quantity.

Highly Overrated

High intelligence is highly overrated, while intellecativity is extremely under-rated.

Complicated Equations

Complicated equations are sideshows in science, because nature is really sim-pletistic.

Supercompressed Air

Someday, cars might run on supercompressed air that is used to generate the mechanical motion of the cars.

Teleportation

Teleportation does not have to occur instantaneously, but it can occur noninstantaneously under the right circumstances.

Simpletism

I believe that nature is simple and uncomplicated, and I call such a belief simpletism.

Most Blacks

Most blacks work very hard, but they are not very productive. In other words, most blacks do not produce a lot of honey, unless they are forced to do so by outside forces, although they work very hard.

Reality Oscillates

Reality oscillates between existence and nonexistence an infinite number of times in each duration of time.

Can Be Altered

Some of the characteristics of certain substances can be altered temporarily as long as the substances are in contact with certain other substances that have special characteristics.

Productive

In order for human beings to be productive and produce a lot of honey, they must be creative and imaginative. In other words, they must be willing and eager to innovate.

The Olympic Games

The Olympic games are really about the struggle among the Gods for control of Mount Olympus.

Vatican Policy

It is Vatican policy that if one wants to be a buller in the Roman Catholic Church, one has to become a member of the clergy, because, otherwise, one cannot be a practicing buller in the Catholic Church.

Predator Animals

Some predator animals are no respecter of human beings, and this is also true of human beings who become predators.

At Any Point

The video camera and video monitor closed-loop memory circuit can be accessed for information removal, storage, and retrieval at any point in the closed loop.

Problems

Problems that most people find easy to solve, I find difficult to solve; while problems that most people find difficult to solve, I find easy to solve.

The Clergy

The clergy is famous for saying that the devil comes in sheep's clothing, but what the clergy does not tell the people is that the clergy wears sheep's clothing.

There Are

There are more things in heaven and earth than are contained within science, philosophy, or religion.

Solipsism

Solipsism is true, because the self is the only conscious being that exists in each person's mind.

Index

0-595-28158-3

www.ingramcontent.com/pod-product-compliance
Lightning Source LLC
Chambersburg PA
CBHW030812180526
45163CB00003B/1251